The Good, the Bad, and the Body:
Body Part Imagery as Patristic Metaphor
for Vice and Virtue

by
Stephen Morris

To borrow an expression anthropologists have used to contrast contemporary non-western religions with post-reform and counter-reform Christianity, medieval religion was not believed but danced. To understand the "steps" of this dance, the archeologist must distinguish the essential structures unifying his material.... This sort of juxtaposition of implicit and explicit meaning is always difficult and subtle. An adequate examination must provide what anthropologist Clifford Geertz calls "thick description," .... [and] follow the function of elements, not in the functionalist-reductionist sense of early twentieth-century English cultural anthropologists but as parts of the larger system of social meaning and process.

... That these [patristic and medieval Christian beliefs and practices] did not conform to post-reform and counter-reformation views of Christianity is immaterial. Medieval religion was neither magic nor religion in the modern sense of these terms. More all-encompassing than modern, compartmentalized religion and less rationalized, codified, and articulated, medieval religion was an expression of a perception of the world, at times through joyous liturgical dance, at times through desperate physical abuse.

> Patrick Geary, *Living With the Dead in the Middle Ages* (pp. 44, 124)

The body is central to the classic Christian understanding of the human person.

There is no complete person without the presence of both body and soul: a soul without a

body is a ghost and a body without a soul is a corpse. The idea of "person" was not

> a concept of soul escaping body or soul using body; it was a concept of self in which physicality was integrally bound to sensation, emotion, reasoning, identity – and therefore finally to whatever one means by salvation. Despite its suspicion of flesh and lust, Western Christianity did not hate or discount the body. Indeed, person was not person without

body, and body was the carrier or the expression (although the two or not the same thing) of what today we call individuality.[1]

When reciting the Nicene Creed, that central statement of Christian faith, the faithful assert belief not in the immortality of the soul but in the resurrection of the dead: the reunion of body and soul which makes life possible in the Kingdom of God. In the early days of the New Testament, St. Paul was already preaching the centrality of the body in Christian experience.

> I appeal to you therefore, brethren, by the mercies of God, to present your bodies as a living sacrifice, holy and acceptable to God, which is your spiritual worship. (Romans 12.1)

> The body is not meant for immorality, but for the Lord, and the Lord for the body. And God raised the Lord and will raise us up by His power. Do you not know that your bodies are members of Christ? ...So glorify God in your body. (I Cor. 6.13-15, 20)

It is the body which is the locus of salvation or damnation, and of those religions that teach resurrection of the body, only "Christianity has defended the idea that body is crucial to self in the most strident and extensive, the most philosophically and theologically confused (and rich) form."[2]

In patristic thought, it is the body which makes mankind superior to the angelic hosts.

> ... God brought into existence mental essence, by which I mean angels and all the heavenly orders.... So He created both the kind of being that is of His own nature (for the nature that has to do with reason is related to God, and apprehensible by mind alone), and the kind which, inasmuch as it clearly falls under the province of the senses, is separated from Him by the greatest interval. And it was also fit that there should be a mixture of both kinds of being, as a token of still greater wisdom and the opulence of

---

[1] Caroline Walker Bynum, *The Resurrection of the Body in Western Christianity, 200-1336.* (New York: Columbia University Press.) 1995. p. 11.
[2] Caroline Walker Bynum, *The Resurrection of the Body*, p. 13.

> the Divine expenditure as regards natures… to be a sort of connecting link between the visible and invisible natures.[3]

As summarized by John of Damascus, God formed mankind's body of earth and the "reasoning and thinking soul" were bestowed by God's own inbreathing.[4] It is man's role as microcosm of the world, uniting in him all the qualities and materials of the visible and invisible orders (with the potential for "becoming deified, in the way of participating in the divine glory")[5] which make him superior to the bodiless hosts of heaven.

This role of the body, in patristic thought, as crucial to the understanding of what makes a human being is what makes the use of body-language and metaphor so important in patristic letters, sermons, commentaries, and other texts. In exploring the imagery of various body parts as metaphor for the human experience of good and evil, the Fathers were exploring basic questions: What is humanity? What does it mean to be a microcosm of the world? How integral to our personhood is our experience of good and evil? Which aspects of our experience and our choices remain temporary/superficial or external to us? Which become eternal/fundamental to our ongoing personality?

Simultaneous with the Fathers' use of body part metaphors was the Christian practice of how bodies were actually handled and treated. The veneration of relics and the attempts to destroy (or at least remove) the remains of the wicked are more than simply background to the Fathers' thought. The basic Christian experience of "body" and notions of how the flesh communicates goodness or evil to the world shaped the experiences and thought patterns of the patristic and medieval thinkers.

---

[3] John of Damascus, *On the Orthodox Faith*. II.12. (Trans. in *Nicene and Post-Nicene Fathers. Second Series,* P. Schaff and H. Wace, eds. vol 9, p. 30. Reprinted by Hendrickson Publishing: Peabody, Massachusetts. 1995. Orig. pub. by Charles Scribner's Sons, 1899.)
[4] John of Damascus, *On the Orthodox Faith*. II.12.
[5] John of Damascus, *On the Orthodox Faith*. II.12.

Pre-industrial societies (including the Mediterranean world of late antiquity) are "governed by personal relationships, not impersonal laws," and either health or "contagion tends to be seen as meaningful and deliberate and its patterns based on values and vendettas, not on genetic predisposition or the domestic accommodations of the rat flea."[6] The ancient mind

> looks, not for the 'how,' but for the 'who,' when it looks for a cause. Since the phenomenal world is a 'Thou' confronting early man, he does not expect to find an impersonal law regulating a process. He looks for a purposeful will communicating an act. If the rivers refuse to rise, it is not suggested that the lack of rainfall on distant mountains adequately explains the calamity. When the river does not rise, it has *refused* to rise. (orig. emph.)[7]

It was the Christian viewpoint that the dead "would not remain dead forever" and that "events, both good and evil, [were ascribed] to [these] persons rather than to fate, fortune, or impersonal magic."[8] God is the ultimate governor of the universe and any power the saints wield was delegated to them by God; the place of saints in early Christian society was not only "a system of beliefs about the dead but an acknowledgement of the dead's place in society"[9] and the power or authority which these dead continued to wield.[10]

The saints were fully present in their body parts, their relics, which were preserved, distributed, and displayed across Europe and the Middle East.[11]

> Here God's grace sets before you the power of the apostles by the great pledges contained in this meagre dust. Here lie father Andrew, the gloriously famed Luke, and Nazarius, a martyr glorious for the blood he

---

[6] Paul Barber, *Vampires, Burial, and Death*. (New Haven: Yale University Press.) 1988. p. 178.

[7] H. and H.A. Frankfurt, *Before Philosophy* (Penguin Books, 1963) cited by Paul Barber, *Vampires, Burial, and Death*, pp. 81-82.

[8] Patrick Geary, *Furta Sacra: Thefts of Relics in the Central Middle Ages*. (Princeton University Press) 1978, revised 1990. pp. 30,31.

[9] Patrick Geary, *Living With the Dead in the Middle Ages*. (Cornell University Press) 1994. p. 43.

[10] Paul Barber, *Vampires, Burial and Death*. p. 196.

[11] See Caroline Walker Bynum, *The Resurrection of the Body*. p. 205.

shed; here are Protasius and his peer Gervasius, whom God made known after long ages to His servant Ambrose.[12]

The relics were the place where the faithful could find the victory of Christ over death made manifest. The relics were the locus of salvation.

> … here [deposited in the altar at Nola] is the cross, joined with those who witnessed to it. For the tiny splinter from the wood of the cross is a mighty promise. The whole power of the cross lies in this small segment. It was brought to Nola by the gift of holy Melania, this greatest of blessings that has come from Jerusalem. The holy altar conceals a twofold honor to God, for it combines the cross and the ashes of the martyrs. How right it is that the bones of holy men lie with the wood of the cross, so that there is rest on the cross for those who died for it![13]

"Jerome coupled an attack on disrespect for asceticism with a defense of relics as the noble places where virtue is achieved."[14] By venerating the relics of the saints – prostrating before them, kissing them or the reliquaries which contained them, or otherwise touching the relics or reliquaries – the faithful were able to touch virtue personified and the divine presence would "rub off" on them as well. Originally venerated in the tombs or cemeteries where they were buried following either martyrdom or peaceful death, these relics were considered so powerful and were so popular, it became customary to divide and "translate" (transfer) them to various other churches or shrines. Sacred thefts were not unheard of either as local people strove to bring talismans, souvenirs, and new patrons home.[15] It was also possible to chastise the saints (if they were derelict in their duty to protect their clients) by the "humiliation" of their relics.[16]

---

[12] Paulinus of Nola, *Epistle* 32.17. trans. available in *Letters of St. Paulinus of Nola, vol. 2*. P.G. Walsh, translator and annotator. (*Ancient Christian Writers, vol. 36*. J. Quasten, W. Burghardt, T. Lawler, eds.) New York: Newman Press. 1967. pp. 150-151.
[13] Paulinus of Nola, *Ep.* 32.11.
[14] Caroline Walker Bynum, *The Resurrection of the Body*. p. 104.
[15] See *passim* Patrick Geary's excellent study, *Furta Sacra: Thefts of Relics in the Central Middle Ages*.
[16] See Lester K. Little's *Benedictine Maledictions: Liturgical Cursing in Romanesque France*. (Ithaca: Cornell University Press.) 1993.

Relics were not simply the bones or other internal body parts of the martyrs or other saints. Any portion or fragment of a saint (including items that had simply been in close proximity to the saints while alive or to their relics after death – the longer or more extensive the contact, the better) was considered a relic capable of passing on virtue and power or of influencing the physical world.

> Eucharius is a presbyter from Spain, living at Calama. He had been suffering from the [kidney?] stone for a longtime; but he was cured by the relics of [St. Stephen the protomartyr], which were brought to him by Bishop Possidius. Later on he was stricken with another disease; the illness grew worse; he was laid out for dead, and his thumbs were already tied together. But the presbyter's tunic was sent to the martyr's shrine; it was brought back and put on his body as he lay there; and by the aid of the martyr the presbyter revived.[17]

The variety of official relic-ranking continues to this day. In the Roman Catholic Church there developed (and continues)[18] the practice of ranking relics as primary, secondary, and tertiary. Primary relics are those which could only be obtained by causing grave harm to the saint, if alive – such as bones, blood, etc. Secondary relics are those which could be obtained from the saint (if alive) without causing grave damage: fingernail or toenail clippings, hair clippings, articles of clothing. Tertiary ("third order") relics are objects which have been touched to or placed in close proximity to a primary or secondary relic. Thus, a piece of wood touched to a primary relic of the True Cross becomes itself a tertiary relic of the Cross. For those poorer pilgrims, these tertiary relics were often the only way they could bring home the presence of the saint or shrine they had visited. (The same practical use of primary, secondary, and tertiary relics continues among Eastern

---

[17] Augustine of Hippo, *City of God* XXII.8. trans. available by Henry Bettenson in *The City of God* (London: Penguin Books.) 1984. p. 1041.
[18] Personal communication from Sister Dorothy Flanagan, CND, Associate Superintendent of Schools for Religious Education of the Archdiocese of New York (December 19, 2000), citing the *Catholic Encyclopedia* (vol. 12, pp. 234-240).

Christians to this day but is not labeled and categorized as neatly as in the West. Relics which Western Christians would categorize as "secondary," such as clothing of St. John of Kronstadt – an early 20th century Russian priest – are displayed in glass cases in Eastern Orthodox churches in Manhattan for the veneration of the faithful, with certificates of authenticity displayed as well.)[19]

It was the physical contact or proximity between relics, or between relics and the living faithful, which made possible the communication of virtue. If the faithful made a pilgrimage to a saint's shrine (such as Thomas Beckett's at Canterbury) in hopes of receiving a healing or message from the saint, the standard practice was to spend the night sleeping in a niche in the saint's shrine or tomb; the relics were to be touched, insofar as this was possible, in order to receive the dream-vision or miracle desired.[20]

If relics of the saints could communicate virtue and strength, the remains of the wicked could bring contagion and death as well. As the world was governed by choices and relationships, not physical laws (by "who," not an impersonal "what"), the disasters and plagues which afflicted families, villages, and continents were the result of anger and feuds of the evil who had departed this life. Contact with their remains was dangerous and so these remains (once identified as the source of the current affliction) were to be destroyed or at least removed from society. The bodies of those considered witches or vampires (much broader – even overlapping – categories of creatures than Hollywood would have us believe) were exhumed, staked, dismembered, scattered, "drowned" in bogs or re-buried at crossroads far from town; if possible, they were to be burned, an

---

[19] The relics of St. John of Kronstadt are displayed in the parish of Christ the Savior on East 71 Street in Manhattan; the royal mantle of Czar Nicholas II is displayed in the cathedral of the Russian Orthodox Church Outside of Russia on east 93 Street.

[20] See Ronald Finucane, *Miracles and Pilgrims: Popular Beliefs in Medieval England*. (New York: St. Martin's Press.) 1977, 1995.

endeavor which took such incredible effort that it was undertaken only as a last measure of desperate resort.[21] (The effort to which the pagan Romans went to dispose of the Christians they martyred is a testimony to how dangerous the Romans understood the Christians to be.

> For they cast to the dogs those who had died of suffocation in prison, carefully guarding them by night and day, lest any one should be buried by us. And they exposed the remains left by the wild beasts and by fire, mangled and charred, and placed the heads of the others by their bodies, and guarded them in like manner from burial by a watch of soldiers for many days.... The bodies of the martyrs, having thus in every manner been exhibited and exposed for six days, were afterwards burned and reduced to ashes, and swept into the Rhone by the wicked men, so that no trace of them might appear on the earth.[22]

Not only did the Christians need to be removed from the society of the living but their remains had to be dissected and burned in order to utterly remove them from influencing the world at all.

The power of these saintly and diabolic body parts shaped the patristic use of body part imagery as they preached and wrote. The body parts they used as poetic metaphor were the same body parts held up for veneration or execration by the faithful. This was what Christian bodies became. If the faithful were to make their own body parts into relics of the saintly and avoid becoming objects to be abused and desecrated, they had best heed the patristic warnings and exhortations to cultivate the virtues in their body parts now, while alive.

Paulinus of Nola (d. 431) was stricken gravely ill sometime in A.D. 399 or 400, cared for by his friend Victor, and recovered. As he described his illness and Victor's

---

[21] See Paul Barber's *Vampires, Burial and Death*, esp. pp. 88, 93, 75-77.
[22] Eusebius, *Ecclesiastical History*, V.i.59, 62. Translation by A. McGiffert in *Nicene and Post-Nicene Fathers (Second Series)*. Eds. P. Schaff and H. Wace. (Peabody, Massachusetts: Hendrickson Publishers.) 1995. (orig. pub. by Christian Literature Publishing Company, 1890.) vol. 1, p. 217.

care for him (in his *Epistle 23*, to Severus), Paulinus had the opportunity to meditate on

the various body parts which Victor had cared for. Paulinus wrote:

> He deigned to cut my hair with his own hands, but desired me to be
> obliged to you for his kindness, for he said that it was at your command
> that he showed his skill. Accordingly I asked him that you should both do
> with earnest prayer what he had done with practiced hand; that you should
> both entreat the Lord that my sins, which are multiplied above the hairs of
> my head [Ps. 40.12] and because of which my soul is unkempt, may not be
> shorn by cutting them [only] halfway, but rather may be cut to the flesh as
> though a razor shaved them.[23]

Paulinus identifies the razor which cuts away the hair and whiskers of his sins as Christ,

enabling him to offer his life "like the hair of the Nazarite [Deut. 21.11] ... consecrate[d]

to God in chastity and thrift."[24] Paulinus advises, however, that his reader must beware

> lest the opposite and hostile razor, which shaved the head of the human
> race in the persons of our first parents who were beguiled by baneful
> deceit, mount our head.... We must watch lest it strip us of spiritual grace
> as though the grace were the hair of the Nazarite.[25]

Paulinus points to the hero Samson in the Book of Judges who was

> invincible while he kept his hair, captured when it was cut off, and
> reinvigorated when it grew afresh. Would that he had been as wise at
> taking precautions against [Delilah] as he was at throttling the lion! ...The
> enemy will mock us if we are robbed of grace as Samson was shorn of his
> hair.[26]

If grace is lost as hair that is shorn, Paulinus points out that it is always possible to repent

and be "made whole with the fresh growth of grace as if [your] hair had grown again."[27]

Paulinus then warms to his subject. "It is pleasant to give free rein to words, and

to follow the strong man of the Lord to his death so that I may weave an entire letter out

---

[23] Paulinus of Nola, *Ep. 23*.10.
[24] Paulinus of Nola, *Ep. 23*.10.
[25] Paulinus of Nola, *Ep. 23*.11.
[26] Paulinus of Nola, *Ep. 23*.11-12.
[27] Paulinus of Nola, *Ep. 23*.13.

of the subject of hair."[28] He reviews the life of Samson as a type (anticipation,

prefiguration) of Christ, returning to the subject of hair a few paragraphs later.

> So I believe that the figure of Samson, renewed in Christ, both with hair
> grown new and in death, is apposite also to every servant of Christ. A man
> who has been overtaken in any fault, once his hair, so to speak, grows
> afresh, returns to salutary repentance to the renewal of grace, and makes
> his arms like a brazen bow....

> Our hair, too, like the yoke is light, for, as Divine Scripture teaches us, the
> hair of holy men is a mark of strength, like Samson's, or of holiness, like
> Samuel's; that of wicked men is a mark of oppression, like Absalom's, or
> of foulness, like Nebuchodnodor's. By this dissimilarity between men and
> between their hair, we are taught to judge men's works by their locks, for
> when the Assyrian king was condemned to the exile of a wild animal, his
> unshorn hair grew grievously stiff and bristled like a lion's mane.[29]

Paulinus points out that Absalom "had a very fine head of hair" but not the strength or

grace of Samson. Quoting the Scriptures, Paulinus explains that Absalom had to cut his

hair because "it was burdensome; and when he was shorn he weighed the hairs of his

head and they weighed [two hundred shekels] according to the royal weight." [II Samuel

14.26][30]

> Could there be a more explicit statement than this that one's hairs are
> numbered according to one's deeds, since Scripture has shown that this
> wicked man's head had no strength but merely a weight of hair? "He
> weighed," says Scripture, "the hairs of his head." For the wicked man, his
> injustice is a source of glory. As someone has said, not merely his wicked
> deeds but also a reputation for wickedness pleases him. So you have the
> verse in Psalms: "Why dost thou glory in malice, thou that art mighty in
> iniquity?" For the light of wicked men is darkness, their glory is a shadow,
> their high position is transitory, their head is the devil, and therefore their
> hair is a dead weight.

> This is why Scripture says that the hair of that murderer was heavy
> "according to the royal weight," in other words by the weight of the
> devil.... The locks of such men are their sins, and therefore theirs cannot
> be the hair by which the consecrated warrior [Samson] broke the bonds of

---

[28] Paulinus of Nola, *Ep. 23*.14.

[29] Paulinus of Nola, *Ep. 23*.17.

[30] Paulinus of Nola, *Ep. 23*.20.

the enemy, and their new ropes as though they were soft threads. Rather, their hair is that of which it is written: "The cords of the wicked have compassed me." For the soul is enmeshed and oppressed by its sins. This view the prophet fully approves when he says: "My iniquities are gone over my head, and as a heavy burden are become heavy on me."[31]

The wickedness of Absalom required shaving and cutting, as it was dragging him down into hell. The loss of his hair had the potential to save him, whereas Samson's loss of hair condemned him to the devil's clutches and only the regrowth of his hair could save him. Continuing his meditation, Paulinus writes:

> You see how heavy the locks of a sinner are. But he whose hair is Christ is light and swift, and he rejoices, saying: "God, who girds me with strength and has made my way blameless, who has made my feet like the feet of harts, and who setteth me in high places." As I have said, the yoke and hair of Christ are light, because by serving Christ we perform the good works by which we wing up to the heights....[32]

Paulinus points out that with his hair/grace restored, the hero had "ceased to long for the recovery of his sight... because the strength of heavenly grace, so healthy in inward vision, did not need bodily sight."[33] Paulinus veers off to discuss sin and righteousness and concludes with St. Paul's proclamation that the heavy Law which leads to sin in the Old Testament has been replaced with the liberty which leads to righteousness in the Gospel.

He resumes the theme of hair when he says,

> So hair was honored whilst the spiritual veil of the Law had to be observed even in bodily appearance; but now it is a burden, since the Sun of eternal freedom has shone forth and Christ has become our head to relieve us of our yoke and of the weight of our bent heads. Therefore as free men we now dare to proclaim with voices of joy and praise: "Let us break their bonds asunder and let us cast away their yoke from us...." The barber has appeared at the apposite time for this moment of grace in which our freedom has shown itself, so that he can lighten me of the all too lengthy

---

[31] Paulinus of Nola, *Ep. 23*.20.
[32] Paulinus of Nola, *Ep. 23*.21.
[33] Paulinus of Nola, *Ep. 23*.21.

covering of my head. So even the body's appearance can attest the benefit of spiritual grace, and a clear uncovered forehead reveal the joy of inner freedom.[34]

Christ the barber appears to shave the burden and sin of the Law from the head of the faithful but the long hair of virtue is always appropriate and is to be cultivated and cared for by the faithful. Picking up on St. Paul's discussion of hair as an image of subjection in I Corinthians 11, Paulinus makes a fascinating aside:

> The Apostle's authority has allowed only women to have long hair, for though their faith like that of men removes the veil from their hearts, fitting modesty demands a covering for their heads and a veil for their brows.... Let them realize why Paul ordered their heads to be clothed with a more abundant covering; it is because of the angels, that is, the angels who are ready to seduce them....
>
> Paul's teaching is relevant here, that a woman ought to cover her head especially in prayer and prophecy. Then she becomes pregnant with the spirit, and accordingly rouses the hatred of the tempter all the more when she leaves behind the boundaries of her womanly weakness, and aspires to human perfection. It is not surprising that Paul has the same view of prayer as prophecy, for elsewhere he says that we pray by the spirit.... So because a woman becomes spiritually pregnant also when she prays, Paul desires her appearance to reveal that she has a power over her head, so that the wiles and snares of the enemy may not confront her.... Her hair shows that by this power she is both guided and defended. Strength is bestowed on her by that very humility of heart by which through the guidance of her self-control she restrains the arrogance of knowledge.... For it will be in vain for her to weigh down her brow with hair if she does not also cover it with modesty.[35]

As an image of faithful obedience and modesty, a woman's long hair becomes a powerful talisman against the Evil One. These tresses proclaim that she is a faithful member of Christ and as a member of His body she is under His divine protection against the machinations of the Devil who would lead her away from Christ and drown her in sin.

---

[34] Paulinus of Nola, *Ep. 23*.23.
[35] Paulinus of Nola, *Ep. 23*.24-25.

Although St. Paul in I Corinthians expects men to have short hair, Paulinus points out that long tresses such as these are appropriate for all the faithful, male and female.

> Let our women have as their hair acts of spiritual virtues, fasting, acts of mercy, prayers. Such hair as this is also fitting for a man. Let Christ's grace, not the grace of their hair, and the precious jewel of chastity, not of costly stones, adorn them…. So let us be eager to be adorned by the hairs of which God keeps count. As He Himself says: "The very hairs of your head are numbered." But on whose head would God deign to number the hairs rather than Christ's, of which He is the head? Of Christ it is said that His head is like *arum cephas*, an expression which I think means a gold of better quality, more pure, like that from the land of Hevilath…. Let us strive, then, with all our resources to prepare ourselves that we may deserve to be the hair and the gold of the divine Head. Christ, by the grace of God, is that Head for us…. [just as] the head of Christ is God, and His hairs are His chosen saints, in whom the Father takes joy in Christ….[36]

Long hair becomes synonymous with grace and beauty, modesty and fidelity in Christ. This is an eschatological vision of the obedient Church in glory with Christ as He shares the glory of the Father. As her members – the saints, each member of the faithful – adorn themselves with the glorious cascading golden locks of virtue (including the liberty of obedience to each other and – ultimately – to Christ) healing, shielding, and protecting them from the deceptions and abuse of the Enemy, she becomes the cascading golden locks of Christ's glory of liberating obedience to the Father.

Christ was said to sit in majesty at the right hand of God. In the parable of the sheep and the goats, the saved were led away to glory on Christ's right hand while the damned were led away to perdition on His left (Matthew 25:31-46). This image of "right hand" as saved and "left hand" as damned is taken up by Paulinus and others as well. By laying hands on the heads and necks of their progeny, the Old Testament patriarchs bestowed blessings on their descendants. Those blessed with the right hand were to receive the greater blessing and so Joseph was shocked when his father Jacob crossed his

---

[36] Paulinus of Nola, *Ep. 23*.24, 26-27, 33.

arms and blessed his eldest grandson Manasseh with his left hand and the younger

grandson Ephraim with the right (Genesis 48:12-22). Paulinus articulated an early

Christian commonplace, that by crossing his arms the patriarch Jacob prefigured the cross

and by blessing Ephraim with his right hand anticipated the demotion of the Old Israel

and the ingathering of the Gentiles into the Kingdom of God.

> The blessing of Ephrem, who was set on the left, but at Jacob's right hand,
> is of profit to us; when Jacob with his arms fashioned the mystery of the
> cross and placed his left hand across to the head of Manasses, who with
> the confidence of the elder brother had taken his position on the right of
> his grandfather, designated for the Jews; for the cross was to them a
> stumbling block, but for the Christians a glory. The cross was to remove
> the Jew from right to left, but me from left to right, for the Jews slipped
> into our wasteland, and we came into their crops. They have taken over
> our blindness, and we have succeeded to their grace.[37]

Paulinus does go on, however, to remind his reader that the Old Israel was only

temporarily moved to the left, so as to make room for the Gentiles; picking up St. Paul's

expectation in the epistle to the Romans, Paulinus also expects the Jews to be regrafted

into the Kingdom.[38]

John Chrysostom (an eastern contemporary of Paulinus) preached on Psalm

110:1, "The Lord says to my Lord: Sit at my right hand....", pointing out to his

congregation:

> Do you see the equality of status? Where there is a throne, you see, there
> is a symbol of kingship; where there is one throne, the equality of status
> comes from the same kingship.... As we do not claim he is greater than
> the Father for having the most honorable seat at his right hand, so you for
> your part do not say he is inferior and less honorable, but of equal status
> and honor. This, in fact, is indicated by the sharing of the seat.[39]

---

[37] Paulinus of Nola, *Ep. 23*.41.

[38] Paulinus of Nola, *Ep. 23*.41.

[39] John Chrysostom, *On the Psalms*, Ps. 110. (trans. by Robert C. Hill in *John Chyrsostom: Commentary on the Psalms, vol. 2.* Brookline, Massachusetts: Holy Cross Orthodox Press. 1998. p. 16.)

Chrysostom underlines "right hand" as a place, a location in (albeit) spiritual geography, in his sermon for Psalm 121:5 ("The Lord will protect you; he is your shelter at your right hand").

> ...He is your defender, [the psalmist] is saying, your ally, your help. Now, in terms of a metaphor of those ranked in battle array, he will take a position at your right hand so that you may be invincible, up and doing, strong, powerful, set up a trophy, carry the day, since it is most of all thanks to this that we shall put everything into operation. He is not only your defender, however, or ally, but also shelter. I repeat: the psalmist expresses God's help by means of things familiar to us, he conveys his total protection and available assistance through right hand and shelter.[40]

The right hand is, for Chrysostom in these sermons, a place where Christ is seated with the Father and where He stands with us, as it is for Paulinus a place where Jews and Gentiles take turns sitting with God as well. More than simply a place, however, the "hand" can be an act or work of God or His servants, such as Moses (in Deuteronomy 34:12) and Psalm 78:42.[41] In Psalm 74:10, the psalmist cries to God who seems to have cast off His chosen: "Why do you draw back your hand? Why is your right hand hidden in your bosom?" Paulinus was aware that "hand" was action as well as place when he wrote:

> Let us also be the right hand of Him who is wholly a right hand; in our actions let us have no left hand so that we may deserve to stand on the right hand of the Judge, or rather, to be His right hand; thus, on the day of retribution, the Lord who repays may count our deeds as the hairs of His head, as he Himself stated in the Gospel.[42]

Hand and hair go "hand-in-hand" here, as action (hand) become virtue (the long hairs to be counted).

---

[40] John Chrysostom, *On the Psalms*, Ps. 121.
[41] Calum Carmichael, *Story of Creation: Its Origin and Interpretation in Philo and the Fourth Gospel.* (Ithaca: Cornell University Press.) 1996. p. 17.
[42] Paulinus of Nola, *Ep. 23*.31.

Chrysostom also uses the image of "hand" to mean "action" in several passages where he extols the need for prayer and virtue in the lives of his parishioners. Preaching on Psalm 141:2, "Let my prayer arise like incense before you, the lifting up of my hands as the evening sacrifice," which was probably sung every dusk at Vespers, he asked,

> Now, how would that [the prayer rising like incense and the lifted hands accepted as the evening oblation in the Temple] happen? If both were pure, if both were spotless, both tongue and hands, the latter cleansed of avarice and rapacity, the former rid of evil words....

> ...what is the meaning of the extension of the hands? Since they minister to many wicked actions, such as beatings, murders, robberies, fraud, for that very reason we are bidden lift them up so that the ministry of prayer may prove a containment of those very vices and freedom from evil. The result will be that whenever you are on the point of robbing or defrauding or striking somebody else, you may recall that you are soon to send those to God in the role of advocate and through them offer that spiritual sacrifice, and not shame them and render them mute by the ministry of evil behavior. So purify them by almsgiving, loving-kindness, patronage of the needy, and in this condition bring them to prayer: if you are not confident of raising them in prayer unwashed, with much less justification would you stain them with sin. If you feared the lesser evil [praying in public with dirty hands], much more should you be horrified at the greater: praying with unwashed hands is not as inappropriate as that, whereas offering them besmirched with countless sins occasions awful anger.[43]

He picks up the same theme as he preaches on Psalm 150:

> So just as [the psalmist] urges the Jews to praise God with all the instruments, so he urges us to do so with all our bodily parts – eye, tongue, hearing, hand.... Hands [praise God] when they reach out not to robbery and greed and violence but to almsgiving and defense of the wronged.[44]

The hands in general, and the right hand in particular, is the act of virtue and charity which wins a place of honor in the Kingdom. To sit at the right hand of the Judge, it is necessary to reach out with love to the neighbor first. But just as salvation can be won by a man's right hand, it can be forfeited by his right hand as well.

---

[43] John Chrysostom, *On the Psalms*, Ps. 141.
[44] John Chrysostom, *On the Psalms*, Ps. 150.

> "Rescue me from the hand of foreign tribes, whose mouths spoke futility and whose right hand is the right hand of unrighteousness" [Psalm 144:7-8].... What could be worse than this, then, turning into a subterfuge what is given to us for assistance? We have right hands, after all, for avenging injustice done to ourselves or others, for doing away with lawlessness, for being a haven and refuge for those wronged. So what excuse would those people have who employ this implement not for the salvation of others but for their own ruin?[45]

When the right hand is used as if it were the left, when strength is used not for righteousness but for selfish gain, then the right hand drags the person into the abyss, where the goats of Matthew 25 perish in misery.

Old age was also utilized as an image to describe both virtue and vice in the life of the believer. The Old Testament assumes that parents and elders would be wise and venerable but the book of Wisdom point out that "old age is not honored for length of time, nor measured by number of years; but understanding is grey hair for men, and a blameless life is ripe old age" (Wisdom 4:8-9). The equation of authentic old age with understanding and purity is repeated by John Cassian (another of Paulinus' contemporaries), quoting the monastic elder Moses the Black:

> Just as all young men are not similarly fervent in spirit and instructed in discipline and the best habits, so neither can all the elders be found to be similarly perfect and upright. For the riches of the elders are not to be measured by their grey hairs but by the hard work of their youth and the desserts of their past labors. For it is said: 'How will you find in your old age what you have not gathered in your youth? For old age is honorable not because of long duration, nor is it computed in terms of number of years, for a man's understanding is grey hair, and a spotless life is old age.' Therefore we should not follow in the footprints of all the elders whose heads are covered with grey hair and whose long life is the only thing that recommends them, nor should we accept their traditions and counsel. Instead we should follow those who we recognize have shaped their lives in a praiseworthy and upright manner as young men, and who have been instructed not in their own presumptions but in the traditions of their forebears. For there are some – and, more's the pity, they are the majority – who have grown old in the lukewarmness and idleness that they

---

[45] John Chrysostom, *On the Psalms*, Ps. 144.

learned in their youth and who claim authority for themselves based not on their mature behavior but on their many years.[46]

Jerome, when writing to Paulinus, urges him

Do not, my dearest brother, estimate my worth by the number of my years. Grey hairs are not wisdom; it is wisdom which is as good as grey hairs. At least that is what Solomon says: 'Wisdom is the grey hair unto men'.... Do not, I repeat, weigh faith by years, nor suppose me better than yourself merely because I have enlisted under Christ's banner earlier than you.... How many there are nowadays who have lived so long that they bear corpses rather than bodies and are like whited sepulchers filled with dead men's bones. A newly kindled heat is more effective than a long continued lukewarmness.[47]

It is the virtue of discretion which is lauded by Abba Moses, John Cassian, and Jerome as the true glory of the elders. It is discretion which wins the admiration and following of those younger in the faith and enables one to serve as a spiritual mentor, a monastic *abba* or *amma*. Old age without discretion is shamefacedness and sin. To be old without discretion is to be part of the "old world which is passing away" (II Cor. 5:17), the fallen kingdom of the "ancient dragon" or the "ancient serpent" (Apoc. 12:9, 20:2), the "ancient kingdom [of evil] which was utterly destroyed" when the Word was made flesh and revealed to the world.[48] Body parts could be old or young depending on the discretion, not the chronological age, of the person.

But perhaps the body parts that most capture the interest of modern folk are genitalia, or "gender" of the body as a whole. The modern stereotype that Christians disparaged genitals and sexuality is too simplistic to be true. Tertullian wrote that all

---

[46] John Cassian, *Conferences*, 2.13.1-3. (trans. by Boniface Ramsey, O.P. in *John Cassian: The Conferences. (Ancient Christian Writers, vol. 57.* eds. J. Quasten, W. Burghardt, T. Lawler. New York: Newman Press. 1997. p. 94.)

[47] Jerome, *Epistle 58*.1. (trans. by W.H. Freemantle, *Nicene and Post-Nicene Fathers (Second Series)*. Eds. P. Schaff and H. Wace. Pebody, Massachusetts: Hendrickson Publishers. 1995. orig. pub. by Christian Literature Publishing Company, 1890. vol. 6, p. 119.)

[48] Ignatius of Antioch, *Epistle to the Ephesians,* 19.3. (trans. by Cyril Richardson in *Early Christian Fathers*, New York: Macmillan Publishing Company. 1970. p. 93.)

organs, including genitalia, are good in and of themselves; it is only our misuse of them that is to be condemned.[49] Jerome praises the use of genitalia (in marriage of course) as, among other things, a source of virgins to populate the monasteries.

> Here also, while we have extolled virginity, we have been careful to give marriage its due. "Had the Lord commanded virginity," we said, "He would have seemed to condemn marriage and to do away with that seed-plot of humanity from which virginity itself springs. Had He cut away the root, how could He have looked for the fruit? Unless He had first laid the foundations, how could He have built the edifice or crowned it with a roof made to cover its whole extent?" If we have spoken of marriage as the root whose fruit is virginity, and if we have made wedlock the foundation on which the building or roof of perpetual chastity is raised… [who] can be so blind as to ignore the foundation…. The apostle casts no snare upon us, nor does he compel us to be what we do not wish. He only urges us to what is honorable and seemly, to be anxious always to please Him, and to look for His will which He has prepared for us to do.[50]

Use of sexual organs to insure the continued population of the world is, in fact, to assist in God's ongoing work of creation and to heed His first commandment to the human race:

> Now the sentence and ordinance of God respecting the begetting of children is confessedly being fulfilled to this day, the Creator still fashioning man… at present man must co-operate in the forming of the image of God, while the world exists and is still being formed; for it is said, "Increase and multiply."[51]

Marriage, always to be "in the Lord," is to be the way to work out one's salvation and it is just as difficult to work out one's salvation as a monastic. However, a married

---

[49] Tertullian, *On the Resurrection of the Flesh*, 61. (trans. by Peter Holmes in *Ante-Nicene Fathers,* vol. 3, pp. 592-3. Eds. A. Roberts and J. Donaldson. Peabody, Massachusetts: Hendrickson Publishers. 1995. orig. published by Christian Literature Publishing, 1895.) See also Caroline Bynum, *The Resurrection of the Body,* p. 37.
[50] Jerome, *Ep.* 48.7.
[51] Methodius of Olympus, *Banquet of the Ten Virgins*, II.i. (trans. by W. R. Clark in *Ante-Nicene Fathers*, vol. 6, p. 313. Eds. A. Roberts and J. Donaldson. Peabody, Massachusetts: Hendrickson Publishers. 1995. orig. published by Christian Literature Publishing, 1886.)

couple who uses marriage as a path to sanctity is as rare as a monastic that uses the desert

to truly grow in humble love and is not turned aside by the temptations of pride.[52]

> It is indeed that such marriages have no thought… [but] to please the Lord? But they are rare: who denies this? And, being, as they are, rare, nearly all the persons who are such, were not joined together in order to be such, but being already joined together became such.[53]

> Whereas, then, all Christians have to guard humility… specially it is becoming that they [virgins] be followers and keepers of this virtue… they must with all watchfulness beware, that it [their virginity] not be corrupted with pride.[54]

> Wherefore what shall we say? Is there any thought which a virgin of God may truly have, by reason of which she dare not to set herself before a faithful woman, not only a widow but even married? ….let not this or that virgin, obeying and fearing God, dare to set herself before this or that woman, obeying and fearing God; otherwise she will not be humble, and "God resisteth the proud!"[55]

Sexuality in marriage is the path by which the couple encounters God, the Other,

which the monastic encounters in practicing hospitality and asceticism. As the monastic

liturgical life developed, sleep was seen as an image of death[56] and the virgin (male or

female) prepared for sleep as for death: asking forgiveness from God and others,[57] prayer

for others,[58] self-examination and confession,[59] prayer for deliverance from Hell;[60] beds

---

[52] Methodius of Olympus, *Banquet*. XI.i.

[53] Augustine of Hippo, *On the Good of Marriage*, 14. (trans. C.L. Cornish, *Nicene and Post-Nicene Fathers (First Series)*, vol. 3, p. 405. Eds. A. Roberts and J. Donaldson. Peabody, Massachusetts: Hendrickson Publishers. 1995. orig. published by Christian Literature Publishing, 1887.)

[54] Augustine of Hippo, *Of Holy Virginity*, 33.

[55] Augustine of Hippo, *Of Holy Virginity*, 45.

[56] *The Lenten Triodion*, trans. by Mother Mary and Archimandrite Kallistos Ware. South Canaan, Pennsylvania: St. Tikhon's Seminary Press. 1994. pp. 511, 664, 666. See also *Orthodox Daily Prayers*. South Canaan, Pennsylvania: St. Tikhon's Seminary Press. 1982. pp. 84-5.

[57] *Service Book of the Holy Orthodox-Catholic Apostolic Church*, trans. by Isabel Hapgood. Englewood, New Jersey: Antiochian Orthodox Christian Archdiocese. 1975. (orig. pub. 1906; reprinted 1922; no place given.) p. 162. See also *A Prayerbook*, Cambridge, New York: New Skete (Monks of the Brotherhood of St. Francis). 1976. pp. 241-2.

[58] Hapgood, *Service Book*, pp. 162-3; also *Prayerbook* (New Skete), pp. 242-3.

[59] *A Monastic Breviary*. West Park, New York: Holy Cross Publications. 1976. p. 13.

[60] *Orthodox Daily Prayers*, p. 84.

(as the most likely location of one's last breath)[61] were identified as coffins[62] and sleep

identified as the image of death from which one would wake at the Last Judgment.[63]

Married couples could see their sleeping together as the image of death as well, when

they would be united with the Other, the Divine, face-to-face in an ecstasy that surpassed

description.[64]

On the other hand, genitalia could be used to not only produce future saints (the

humble of every generation) but to pass on the curse of sin and death itself.

> ... whilst, by the generation of the flesh only that sin is contracted which
> is original....[65]
> He [St. Paul] sets forth that this absolute weakness [of sin], or rather
> condemnation, of carnal generation is from the transgression of original
> sin, when ... [he] says that "man that is born of a woman hath but a short
> time to live and is full of wrath." Of what wrath, but of that in which all
> are, as the apostle says, "by nature," that is, by origin, "children of wrath,"
> inasmuch as they are children of concupiscence of the flesh and of the
> world? He further shows that to this same wrath pertains to the death of
> man....[66]

Genitals can be used to produce saints or sinners, the humble as well as the arrogant

cursed with death. Concupiscence (self-love, love of pleasure) and love of God can both

be rooted in and expressed by the use of the sexual organs.

Gender itself, as a way of being, was explored as revealing wickedness and

sanctity as well. Masculinity expressed anger, spirituality, or self-giving while femininity

---

[61] Philippe Aries, *The Hour of Our Death*. Oxford: Oxford University Press. 1981. pp. 14-19, 107-8.

[62] *Orthodox Daily Prayers*, p. 84.

[63] *Orthodox Daily Prayers*, p. 85; see also Philippe Aries, *Hour of Our Death*, pp. 22-4.

[64] Augustine of Hippo, *City of God*, 14.16.(trans. by H. Bettenson, *St. Augustine: Concerning the City of God Against the Pagans*. London: Penguin Books. 1984. p. 577). See also Augustine, *On the Morals of the Catholic Church*, 1.22.40. (trans. in *Nicene and Post-Nicene Fathers*, vol. 4, p. 53); Paulinus of Nola, *Epistle* 23.42; Ilias the Presbyter, *Gnomic Anthology*, IV.72. (trans. by G.E.H. Palmer, P. Sherrard, K. Ware in *The Philokalia: The Complete Text*. London: Faber and Faber. 1981. vol. 2, pp. 56-7); St. Peter of Damascus, *Third Stage of Contemplation* and *Eighth Stage of Contemplation* (trans. in *The Philokalia*, vol. 2, pp. 120, 142); Methodius of Olympus, *Banquet*, II.ii.

[65] Augustine of Hippo, *On Forgiveness of Sins, and Baptism*, i.20. (trans. by Peter Holmes in *Nicene and Post-Nicene Fathers (first Series)*, vol. 5, p. 22.

[66] Augustine of Hippo, *On Forgiveness of Sins, and Baptism*, ii.15; see also i.9 and iii.15.

expressed *luxuria*, compulsive or predatory sexuality, carnality, or self-giving as well.

The Greek patristic exegesis of Galatians 3:28 ("in Christ there is neither … male nor female"), Maximus the Confessor (in A.D. 628-30) identified "male" and "female" as anger (*thumos*) and lust (*epithumia*).

> …"there is neither male nor female," that is there is neither anger nor desire. Of these, the first tyrannically perverts judgment and makes the mind betray the law of nature; while the second scorns the dispassionate cause and nature, that alone is truly desirable, in favour of what is inferior, giving preference to the flesh rather than to the spirit, and taking pleasure more in visible things than in the magnificence and glory of intelligible realities.[67]

Anger was given to mankind as a force to use in defense of the poor and oppressed (as were right hands) and to "fight to attain our object," whether spiritual or temporal.[68] Anger was, however, too often misdirected and used to defend oneself or provoke others rather than defend the needy.

> … let our [anger] struggle to keep guard over our attachment to Him. Or, more precisely, let our whole intellect be directed towards God, tensed by our [anger] as if by some nerve, and fired with longing by our desire at its most ardent.[69]

> The sins of [anger] are heartlessness, hatred, lack of compassion, rancor, envy, murder and dwelling constantly on such things.[70]

Maximus identified femininity as "desire" or "lust" (*epithumia*), or as the Latins would say, with concupiscence and *luxuria*. *Luxuria* (a better word than modern English "lust" which is too one-dimensional with its identification as simply sexual desire) was "an inordinate craving for carnal pleasure,"[71] any carnal, i.e. material, pleasure. It

---

[67] Maximus the Confessor, *On the Lord's Prayer* (trans. in *The Philokalia*, vol. 2, p. 293).
[68] Maximus the Confessor, *On the Lord's Prayer.*
[69] Maximus the Confessor, *On the Lord's Prayer.*
[70] John of Damascus, *On the Virtues and the Vices* (trans. in The Philokalia, vol. 2, p. 337).
[71] Katherine Ludwig Jansen, *The Making of the Magdalen*. Princeton: Princeton University Press. 2000. p. 164.

included sexual acts but also involved wanting "an excess of just about anything:" make-up, fancy hairstyles, jewelry, perfumes, fine clothing, excessive singing/laughter/chatter, caressing.[72] It was, finally, the uncontrolled desire for any expensive "luxury items" available at the time and the physical titillation that came fast on the heels of possessing them.[73] It was an infectious disease spread primarily by women.[74] This *luxuria* was seen as the root of almost all other sin or tragic circumstance of the human condition.[75] In the spiritual manuals and later confessors' handbooks, *luxuria* was often treated in the chapter concerning pride; *luxuria* was an aspect of the attitude which drove Adam from paradise in the beginning.[76] Women were seen as the sexual predators of society (in contrast to modern assumptions of male sexual insatiability).[77] Most early treatises on virginity are addressed to women; is this because women needed more encouragement to persevere in chastity? Was virginity praised so highly because it was a greater achievement for such sexually compulsive creatures as women to maintain virginity? Or both?

Paulinus also considered the pairing of masculine/feminine in terms of spirituality/carnality, with women assuming the role of the earthly and the fleshly.[78] But women and femininity were the means by which salvation, as well as destruction, came into the world. The Mother of God was seen as the antithesis of the first virgin, Eve, and in the giving of herself Mary set right what Eve had knocked off-track.

> … and [the power of] that seduction by which the virgin Eve, already
> betrothed to a man, had been wickedly seduced was broken when the

---

[72] Katherine Ludwig Jansen, *The Making of the Magdalen,* p. 165.
[73] Katherine Ludwig Jansen, *The Making of the Magdalen,* pp. 161-4.
[74] Katherine Ludwig Jansen, *The Making of the Magdalen,* pp. 169, 173.
[75] Katherine Ludwig Jansen, *The Making of the Magdalen,* p. 254.
[76] Katherine Ludwig Jansen, *The Making of the Magdalen,* p. 164.
[77] Katherine Ludwig Jansen, *The Making of the Magdalen,* pp. 165, 170.
[78] Paulinus of Nola, *Ep. 23*.11-12.

angel in truth brought good tidings to the Virgin Mary, who already [by her betrothal] belonged to a man. For as Eve was seduced by the word of an angel received the glad tidings that she would bear God by obeying his Word. The former was seduced to disobey God [and so fell], but the latter was persuaded to obey God, so that the Virgin Mary might become the advocate of the virgin Eve. As the human race was subjected to death through [the act of] a virgin, so it was saved by a virgin, and thus the disobedience of one virgin was precisely balanced by the obedience of another.[79]

Women as sources of destruction and as saviors appear throughout European fairy tales as well; the ambivalence or liminality of femininity is a basic image in the human experience.

It is the females – the stepmother and the witch – who are the inimical forces in this story. Gretel's importance in the children's deliverance reassures the child that a female can be a rescuer as well as a destroyer.[80]

(Not only *Hansel and Gretel* but *Snow White, Cinderella, Sleeping Beauty* and others show the feminine as source of death – the wicked queen, evil stepmother, wicked witch/fairy – as well as savior – the good fairy, the [fairy] godmother, the faithful young girl.)

Just as woman, the feminine, could give herself to save the world, so could the masculine. Masculinity (summarized in the images of "groom" and "father") was given to the world to protect and give of himself to the point of self-sacrifice.

Husbands, love your wives, as Christ loved the church and gave himself up for her.... Even so husbands should love their wives as their own bodies. He who loves his wife loves himself. For no man ever hates his own flesh, but nourishes and cherishes it, as Christ does the church, because we are members of his body. (Ephesians 5:25, 28-30)

This is especially so if out of ignorance or pride they think that such an awesome task [spiritual fatherhood] involves no danger of condemnation, imagining that it will bring them honor or ease, and not realizing that they

[79] Irenaeus of Lyons, *Adv. Haereses* (trans. by C. Richardson in *Early Christian Fathers*, p. 391).
[80] Bruno Bettelheim, The Uses of Enchantment. (New York: Vintage Books /Random House.) 1989. (orig. pub. 1975) p. 164.

will rather be required, when the moment comes, to enter into an abyss of humility and death for the sake of their spiritual children and their enemies.[81]

What does all this say to us? That the fourth-fifth century fathers hated corporeality? That they hated women? That they were confused in using the same images for so many different things?

The body parts discussed here are associated with the virtues and vices considered most basic to human life. The survival of the community (either secular or ecclesiastical), as well as the survival of the self, depended on these virtues overcoming these particular vices.

Virtue	Vice	Body part
Wisdom, discretion	Foolishness, gossip	Old age
Defense of the needy	Theft, exploitation	Right hand
Love of God, obedience	Love of self	Hair
Self-sacrifice with patience, self-control	Selfishness, with anger, *luxuria*	Gender
Meet God, assist God with ongoing creation	Hedonism	Genitalia

Man (personally and collectively) was considered a microcosm of the world; the world was man writ large. If any one of these vices grew out of control, the society could not function as mistrust, greed, and power ran riot in the streets. Any single person consumed by one of the vices would destroy himself as he destroyed his ties to the

---

[81] St. Peter of Damascus, *Spurious Knowledge*. (trans. avail in *The Philokalia*, vol. 3, p. 196.)

society (both civil and ecclesial) around him. The fate of the cosmos – or at least this

corner of it, where I am – depends on my choices for wickedness or righteousness. The

behavior of villagers or of a neighborhood concerning the bodies of the dead in their

midst attest to this, as they strove to be rid of the corpse of a witch or venerate the corpse

of a saint as each brought either health/salvation or plague/bad weather/disaster to the

area as a result of their choices during life. These bodies and body parts were multi-level,

polyvalent symbols.

> Symbols … defy scholarly attempts to be objective and descriptive
> because they are polyvalent and therefore ambiguous…. Just as there are
> many different signs [words] for one meaning, there may be many
> different meanings for one symbol. Bread, for example, is a symbol in
> many cultures, regardless of the word-sign by which it is called. As such,
> it may evoke a wide range of feelings and responses within the culture in
> which it is used. That it is a cultural phenomenon also means that it is
> related to other symbols and structures in the society in ways hidden from
> the external observer. Moreover, some parts of the symbol may be feelings
> which members of the culture do not formulate as meanings or
> definitions…. Such a symbol can touch deep, unexpressed feelings …
> implicit meanings.

> Someone who has been socialized in a culture may know the symbol in its
> many meanings as only a native can. When the native attempts, however,
> to describe the many things which the symbol means, he or she begins a
> process… which moves the symbol from the realm of polyvalence (where
> it can mean many things simultaneously) to the realm of lexical definition
> (where it can mean many things, but only one at a time). A symbol may
> even "mean" two contradictory things at once – a fact which may only
> become evident when the symbol is "defined." Then what is a bearable
> paradox in the realm of symbol may come to seem illogical and
> untenable….[82]

The fathers of the fourth, fifth, and eighth centuries we have examined here were

socialized in a Christian culture which used symbol and the "free association" of poetry

as naturally as they breathed air. Each body part they described is an ambiguous, living

---

[82] Tia Kolbaba, *The Byzantine Lists: Errors of the Latins*. (Urbana, Illinois: University of Illinois Press.) 2000. p. 105.

mystery which does not "merely point to its referent but actually embodies, participates in, or even constitutes the referent in some physical way."[83] Thus, for Paulinus, a woman's long hair *was* her virtue, protecting her from demons; in the sixties, a teenager's long hair *was* his rebellion. The body parts of each Christian would, when raised at Judgment Day, reveal the truth of his inner dispositions and motivations.

Desire shapes action. As the soul moves to embrace either good or evil, the hand or other appropriate body part follows. Interior virtue and vice shape exterior action and, in the opinion of the fathers, exterior appearance as well. Furthermore, the Good was, by definition, beautiful and beauty was expected to be one of the four basic attributes of the bodies of the saved. In the resurrection, therefore, everyone might have long hair but only the saints' hair would be long, beautiful, luxuriant, and well-cared for; the long hair of the wicked would be matted, tangled locks. In the resurrection, all will have right hands but the right hands of the saved will be strong and firm; the right hands of the damned will be gnarled, arthritic talons. The righteous will be raised in their ripe old ages, rosy, strong and upright, confident; the evil will be raised humpbacked and twisted as decrepit, weak elderly. The sexual organs of the saints will be fruitful and life-giving while the sexual organs of the wicked will be diseased, infected, and contagious, spreading sin (the ultimate STD!) and death. The long hair, right hands, age, genitalia, and gender of each will be seen for what they truly are: beautiful expressions of sanctity and communion with God or hideous cesspools of contagion and sin waiting to infect those around them. The body parts metaphors are capable of expressing many aspects of a personality before death (because evil and goodness are constantly fluctuating realities in a life, not static and frozen; because a human had a body and could therefore repent – unlike the fallen

---

[83] Tia Kolbaba, *The Byzantine Lists,* p. 106.

angels – the quality of good an devil expressed by a person's body parts are in constant ebb and flow)[84] and will be crystallized into signs of the person's basic inclinations and choices when raised. Body parts will – in the meantime – be both good and evil.

That is why the debates and controversies concerning the resurrection body were so important to the theologians of the Middle Ages. How will the body be raised? What will it express? How will salvation or damnation be experienced as a result? It is a matter of eternal life and death.

---

[84] John of Damascus, *On the Orthodox Faith*, II.3-4.

Made in the USA
Middletown, DE
18 December 2021

56553853R00018